How Many Cubs?

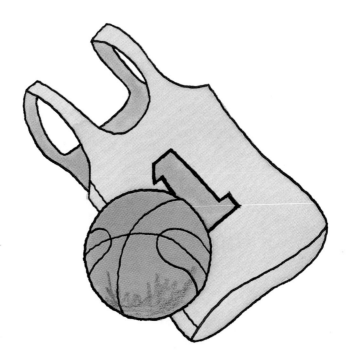

written by Penelope Jones
illustrated by Stan Tusan

 McGraw-Hill
School Division

New York   Farmington

It was time for the big game.

The cubs met in the locker den.

"Many pals have come to see us play," said Peep.

"Are we all together?" asked Kathleen.

"I think we are," said Lee.

"I will count us," said Ben. "Let's line up."

They all lined up. "One . . . two . . .
three . . . four. One cub is missing,"
said Ben.

"We need five cubs and I see
four."

"I think you missed a cub," said Peep.

"Then I will do it again. So keep in line," said Ben

"I see Ted," said Ben. "That's one. I see Peep. Peep is two. Kathleen is three, and Lee is four. One of us is still missing."

"Do it over," said Peep.

"No," said Lee, "this time I will
do it!"

"Good," said Kathleen. "We will
line up."

So all the cubs got into a line
again. Ben was next to Kathleen.
Kathleen was next to Peep, and
Peep was next to Ted. "One . . .
two . . . three . . . four," said
Lee. "I see four. A cub is
missing."

"This is not good," said Peep. "If we are not all together, we can't play."

"Maybe standing in a line is not good. Let's get in a circle," said Ted.

Ben said, "I think we can do this together. Tell how many you see."

"One . . . two . . . three . . . four," said the five cubs.

The cubs were very upset. They did it over and over again. But they always saw four cubs.

"I don't think we can play the game," said Ben. "We must tell our pals to go."

Then Ben looked into the mirror.
"Now I see all of us," he said.
"One . . . two . . . three . . .
four . . . FIVE!"

"Five?" said Lee.

"Yes," said Ben. "Look! Can you
see the five of us?"

"One . . . two . . . three . . .
four . . . FIVE!" said Peep.

"We are all here," said Ben.
"Now we can play in the game!"

"Let's go!" said Ted.